Science Matters
WEDGES

Tatiana Tomljanovic

WEIGL PUBLISHERS INC.

Published by Weigl Publishers Inc.
350 5ᵗʰ Avenue, Suite 3304, PMB 6G
New York, NY USA 10118-0069
Website: www.weigl.com

Library of Congress Cataloging-in-Publication Data

Tomljanovic, Tatiana.
  Wedges / Tatiana Tomljanovic.
      p. cm. -- (Science matters)
  Includes index.
  ISBN 978-1-60596-037-1 (hard cover : alk. paper) -- ISBN 978-1-60596-038-8 (soft cover : alk. paper)
  1. Wedges--Juvenile literature. I. Title.
  TJ1201.W44T65 2010
  621.8--dc22

                              2009001936

Printed in China
1 2 3 4 5 6 7 8 9 13 12 11 10 09

                              Editor Nick Winnick
                    Design and Layout Terry Paulhus

Photograph Credits

Weigl acknowledges Getty Images as its primary image supplier for this title.

What is a Wedge?

Wedges can be found all around you. When people cut logs for a campfire, they use an axe. An axe is a type of wedge. Other types of wedges include any object with a blade, such as a knife or a shovel. Door stops and wheel blocks are types of wedges that can help stop heavy objects from moving.

A wedge is a triangle-shaped tool with a sharp edge. It can be used to separate two objects, lift an object, or hold an object in place.

■ Wedges are one of six simple machines. People use simple machines to make daily tasks easier.

Contents

How do Wedges Work?

In order for a wedge to work, it must be moved. Simple wedges, such as axes, can be moved by hand.

When a wedge is pushed between two objects, the shape of the wedge changes the direction of the push. As the wedge is pushed forward, the thin blade of the wedge is followed by the wider back edge. As the wider part of the wedge is pushed into the material, the wedge begins to press outward. Eventually, this side-to-side **force** splits the objects apart. This outward direction is **perpendicular** to first push on the wedge.

For example, when chopping wood, the downward force of the axe cuts down into the wood. As the axe moves into the wood, it pushes the wood to either side of the blade. This perpendicular force splits the log in two.

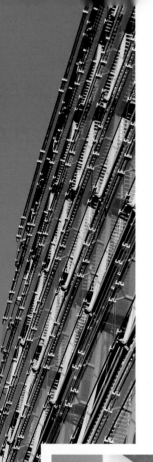

Wicked Wedges

People often confuse wedges with another simple machine, the **inclined plane**. Inclined planes are wedge-shaped structures, such as ramps, that make moving heavy objects easier.

Wedges are inclined planes that can be moved. The wedge moves, and the object the wedge is working on does not. Wedges are commonly used to cut objects. Chefs cut vegetables and other foods with knives, which are a type of wedge. The food remains still while the wedge moves.

■ Wedges are common tools in many careers, from cooking to construction.

Where are Wedges?

Wedges are some of the most commonly used simple machines.

Did you know that scissors are a set of simple machines working together? These sets are called complex machines. The handles of a pair of scissors are simple machines called **levers**. The blades of the scissors are wedges that press against each other. When the scissors close, the wedges on the blades cut apart the object between them.

Wedges are used in many places. They are used in factories to cut material from plastic to metal. Nails have wedge-shaped tips. They can hold objects together or punch precise holes.

Which Wedge is Which?

All wedges have the same basic triangle shape. However, the height and width of that triangle can change. The shape of a wedge depends on the job it needs to do.

Wider wedges push objects apart more easily. Narrow wedges may cut into materials more easily, but they do not push outward with the same force. How well a wedge separates one object from another is called its **mechanical advantage**.

■ In order for most wedges to work well, their edges must be kept sharp.

The Why of Wedges

Most wedges are short and wide rather than long and narrow.

In most cases, it is easier to cut a material with a long, narrow wedge. However, there are problems with that design. Long, narrow wedges are more likely to get stuck in stretchy or rough materials, such as rubber or wood. Knife-like blades can also break easily when working with a tough material like wood. Thicker wedges, such as axes, can be harder to use, but are much less likely to break or become stuck.

A Wedge of History

People have been using wedges to make work easier for a very long time. Scientists have found tools using wedges that are 9,000 years old.

In ancient Egypt, bronze wedges were used to break off blocks of rock for use in building. American Indians often used obsidian, a type of black, glass-like rock, to make both axes and arrowheads.

Early farmers dug their fields with wooden or metal plows pulled by farm animals. The plow is a kind of wedge that is dragged through soil to loosen it. Seeds were easier to plant in the loose soil.

● The plow, a type of wedge, has been used by farmers for thousands of years.

Wedges Through Time

The wedge is one of the oldest tools used by humans. Over time, people have discovered new and different uses for this ancient tool.

- 8000 BC: American Indians use stone wedges for cutting and hunting.

- 500 AD: Farmers attach wheels to plows.

- 1634: Galileo Galilei becomes the first person to write that simple machines do not create **energy**. They only change its strength and direction.

- 1837: John Deere produces the self-polishing plow, which helped farmers deal with tough grasses on the North American prairies.

- 1917: Gideon Sundback invents the modern-day zipper. At the time, it was known as a separable fastener.

- 1929: Army Lieutenant Colonel Jacob Schick **patents** the first electric razor sold in stores.

Complex Machines

Simple machines can be combined together. These combinations can make work easier and faster than any one simple machine on its own. Wedges are an important part of many complex machines.

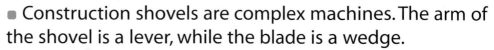
■ Construction shovels are complex machines. The arm of the shovel is a lever, while the blade is a wedge.

Wedges at Work

Jackhammer

A jackhammer is used to break up hard surfaces, such as roads and sidewalks. A jackhammer has a narrow, wedge-shaped blade. The motor in the jackhammer makes the blade hit the concrete many times over. This breaks up the hard surface.

Zipper

A zipper has two rows of teeth that fit together to form a seam. The teeth are pushed together and pulled apart by a slider. Inside the slider are three wedges. When the slider is pulled down, a wedge at the top pushes the teeth apart. When the slider is pulled up, two wedges on the outer edge push the teeth together.

Electric Razor

The electric razor has many blade-like wedges. The motor moves the blades back and forth to cut hair.

Wedges in Your World

Wedges are used every day. They are part of complex machines, but they are also useful by themselves. Small, narrow, wooden wedges are placed under doors to keep them open. Nails hold the walls of a house together.

■ The wedge of a snowplow blade keeps roads clear of snow in winter.

Wedges in Your Head

Some parts of the human body work like simple machines. Wedges can be seen every time you smile.

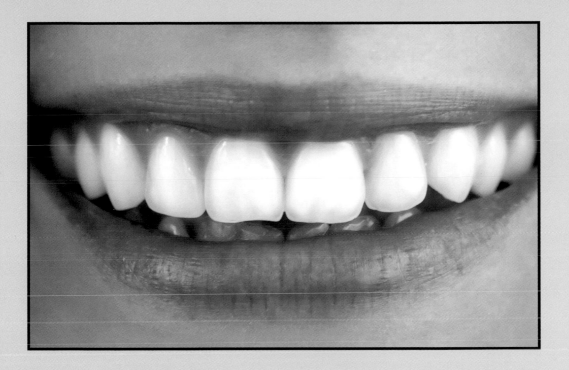

Human teeth are made up of both wide and narrow wedges. The front teeth are long, narrow wedges. They can cut easily through soft food, like chicken or a peach. The back teeth have many short, wide wedges. These are useful for breaking up harder foods, such as nuts or apples.

Wedges and Stone

In the middle ages, most kings and queens lived in castles. Castles were built to be safe from enemy attack. They had to be strong and were made mostly of stone.

Stonemasons are people who make objects out of stone. Stonemasons used hammers and chisels to break off large pieces of stone for building blocks for castles. A chisel is a type of wedge.

The sharp part of a chisel is placed on a stone. The blunt end is hit with a hammer. The force of the hammer hitting the chisel cuts the stone.

■ Large castles were made of thousands of stone blocks, each shaped by chisels.

The Way of the Wedge

Sculptors have used chisels to shape stone for thousands of years. Using a simple wedge, these artists are able to create incredible works or art. Some of these sculptures have stood for many centuries.

Gaining an Advantage

There are six simple machines. They are *inclined planes*, *levers*, *pulleys*, *screws*, *wedges*, and the *wheel and axle*. All simple machines are designed to make work easier. These machines do not have batteries or motors. They do not add any energy of their own to help people do work. So, how do simple machines work?

Simple machines work by changing the forces that are applied to them. In most cases, they do this by changing the distance or direction of a force.

Inclined Planes

Inclined planes are sloping surfaces that connect a lower level to a higher level or the opposite.

Lever

A lever is a moveable bar that rests on a solid point called the fulcrum.

Pulley

A pulley is a wheel with a groove around the outside edge. In this groove, there is a rope or cable. Pulling the rope turns the wheel.

Screw

Screws are tube-shaped tools with sharp edges spiralling around them. They are often used to fasten objects together.

Wedge

A wedge is a triangle-shaped tool with a sharp edge. It can separate two objects, lift an object, or hold an object in place.

Wheel and Axle

Wheels are circle-shaped objects that rotate around their center. They often have an axle in the middle to hold them in place.

Surfing Simple Machines

How can I find more information about wedges and other simple machines?
- Libraries have many interesting books about simple machines.
- Science centers can help you learn more about force, wedges, and complex machines through hands-on experiments.

Test your knowledge of wedges and other simple machines.
Edheads
www.edheads.org
- Click on the simple machines button on the left side of the screen, and then on the "click here to start" to play a virtual game.

Can you identify different types of wedges?
www.mikids.com/Smachines.htm
- Click on wedges, and then try to match the names of different wedges with their pictures.

Science in Action

Working with Wedges

Wedges come in handy when trying to fix everyday problems, such as evening out a wobbly chair or table. Try fixing a wobbly chair or table to see a wedge in action.

You will need:

* a wobbly chair, table, or desk
* a piece of paper

1. Find a chair or desk that does not sit evenly on the floor.
2. Fold a piece of paper in half four or five times.
3. Try placing the piece of paper under each chair leg.

Did you put the folded edge or the loose edges of the paper under the wobbly leg of the chair? Did the paper wedge help to steady the chair?

What Have You Learned?

1 What is a wedge?

2 How many simple machines are there?

3 What sort of wedge does a sculptor or a stonemason use?

4 Who was Gideon Sundback?

5 Name at least three tools that are wedges.

6 What is a plow?

7 In science, what is the definition of work?

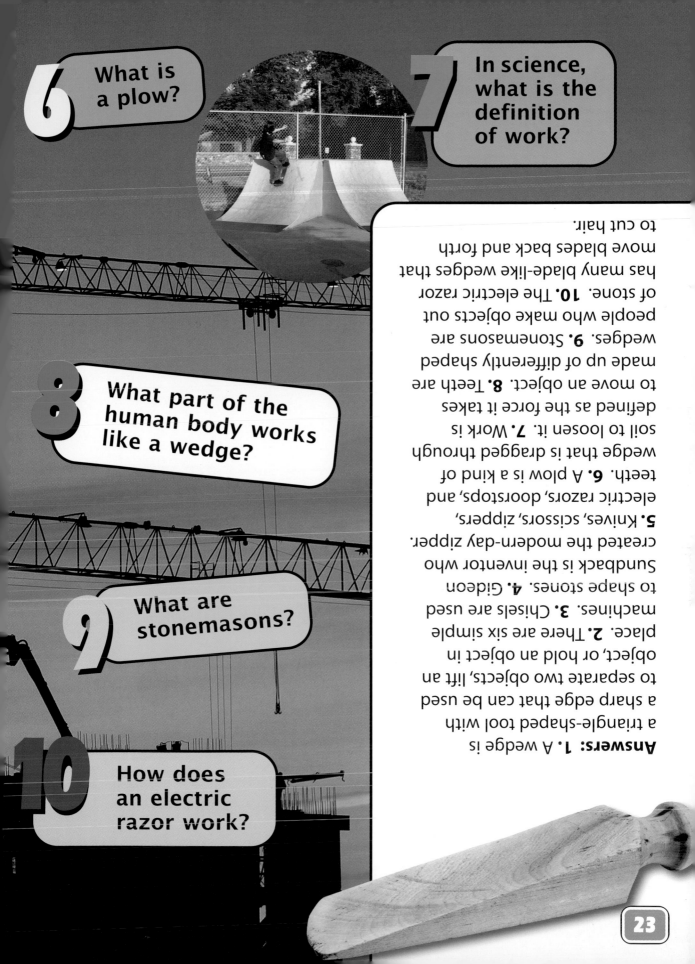

8 What part of the human body works like a wedge?

9 What are stonemasons?

10 How does an electric razor work?

Answers: 1. A wedge is a triangle-shaped tool with a sharp edge that can be used to separate two objects, lift an object, or hold an object in place. **2.** There are six simple machines. **3.** Chisels are used to shape stones. **4.** Gideon Sundback is the inventor who created the modern-day zipper. **5.** Knives, scissors, zippers, electric razors, doorstops, and teeth. **6.** A plow is a kind of wedge that is dragged through soil to loosen it. **7.** Work is defined as the force it takes to move an object. **8.** Teeth are made up of differently shaped wedges. **9.** Stonemasons are people who make objects out of stone. **10.** The electric razor has many blade-like wedges that move blades back and forth to cut hair.

Words to Know

energy: power needed to do work

force: the pushing or pulling on an object

inclined plane: a simple machine with a smooth, slanted surface

levers: moveable bars that rest on a solid point

mechanical advantage: a measure of how much easier a task is made when a simple machine is used

patents: asks for a grant from a government to make, use, or sell something over certain period of time

perpendicular: at right angles to a given line or plane

Index